I0004712

Printed in the United States of America
First Printing, 2015

ISBN-13: 978-1511630238
ISBN-10: 151163023X

WHMCS Limited
Woodside House
Broadway Avenue
Giffard Park
Milton Keynes
MK14 5QF
United Kingdom

www.whmcs.com

1 | **Contents**

Contents

1: Basic Web Hosting Terminology

So, you want to start a web hosting company?

That's a GREAT CHOICE, in our opinion.

This guide is here to help you learn what goes into becoming a host and how to be successful in this fast-growing industry.

> *It will be a lot harder, more challenging and more fun than you ever imagined.*
>
> *- Ken Brubacher, Megaspace Web Hosting*

We are going to cover everything you need to know, from how to pick a server to what information you will need to be able to sell your business once you get successful.

This is not a technical guide. We are not going to walk you through every mouse-click and every option on every menu, but rather see this as a map to show you where you need to go to reach your goal of becoming a successful web hosting company.

Throughout this guide, you will find quotes from other web hosts who have been there already and want to

share some of the knowledge and wisdom they have gained with you.

Before we get started though, let's go over some of the industry terms that you will hear and see bandied about all over the place, just to get us on the same page. (For a more extensive list of terms, see the glossary at the end of the book)

The first, obviously, is **hosting**, or **web hosting**.

Web hosting is the business of providing server space to clients who want to ensure their websites are online 24/7.

It is called hosting because you are providing the technology required, and are acting as a 'host' for your clients' data in this online party we call the Internet.

Control panel: for our purposes, a control panel is the software provided by you, the host, to give the user access to their hosting space. This panel enables them to carry out administrative and maintenance tasks. There are many control panels available, but the main ones we will be talking about in this book are WHM and cPanel. We will also be introducing you to WHMCS, which is a billing software. WHMCS is the most popular and widely used billing automation software in the web hosting

industry today. Your clients will most likely also have separate control panels (dashboards) for their websites such as the WordPress admin panel. One stumbling block that many clients come across is that they do not understand the difference between their hosting control panel and their website's control panel.

WHM: The Web Host Manager (WHM) is the back-end tool for web hosts to manage their servers and the clients that are hosted on it.

cPanel: The other side of the coin from WHM is cPanel, which is the client-side control panel for web servers. While WHM is used to create hosting accounts, cPanel is used to access and manage those accounts.

WHMCS: The Web Hosting Manager Complete Solution (WHMCS) is the world's leading web hosting automation platform. Handling customer signups, provisioning, billing and support, WHMCS is used by tens of thousands of web hosting businesses around the world to manage their daily operations and put them firmly in control of their business.

Hosting plan: A hosting plan defines the facilities on a server made available to an individual website. Generally speaking, each domain name requires its own hosting

plan, which allocates server resources such as disk space, bandwidth, and a variety of other variables including the number of email addresses that can be created and what add-ons are available.

Domain Names: The internet works (from a human standpoint) around a system of domain names. These domain names are often referred to as website addresses. For instance, WHMCS.COM is a domain name, but most people would call it the website address of the WHMCS website. Calling it a web address is a little inaccurate, but it is a description most people can understand.

Domain Registry: All domain names have to be registered with a central registry to ensure that each name is unique and only allocated to one person. There is no single registry for all domain names, but rather they are managed by a series of registries, one for each domain extension (i.e. .com, .ca, .co.uk). Anyone wishing to register a domain name must do so through the services of a registrar.

Domain Registrar: A domain registrar is an agent of a domain registry who has permission to manage the registration of new domain names and the renewal/update of current ones. There are many different registrars, some of whom resell their services to other providers through

the creation of reseller accounts. As a result, there are thousands of companies through whom you can register and maintain domain names. See Chapter 4 for more details on domain registration.

Reseller Account: A reseller account is something which enables a person or business to sell a product or service which is actually provided by a third party. For instance, a hosting reseller account allows you to sell space on someone else's server. They sell the space to you and you 'resell' it to someone else.

Bandwidth: The term, "Bandwidth" can be confusing because it is used in two different ways.

Some people use the term to describe how fast data can be transferred. The faster the transfer rate, the higher the bandwidth. Picture a pipe that data is flowing through like water. The wider the pipe, the greater the amount of water (data) that can go through at one time.

Bandwidth is also (more commonly) used as a measurement of how much data has been transferred over a given time period. In basic terms, the size of each file and the number of times those files have been transferred are totaled up to calculate the total amount of da-

ta transferred - and this is called the amount of band-width used.

Disk Usage: Every file and every piece of data in a website must be stored somewhere and therefore takes up some physical space on a server's hard disks. Disk usage is measured in bytes, with 1024 bytes making a kilobyte (Kb), 1024 kilobytes making a megabyte (Mb) and 1024 megabytes making a gigabyte (Gb). Your servers must have enough physical hard disk space to hold all of the software required to run them, plus all the data your users need to store. Storage space can be allocated per domain and is measured as disk usage.

Datacenter: A datacenter is a building specifically designed and built to house servers. Datacenters are designed with redundant power systems, fire protection and multiple internet connections to attempt to ensure that, whatever the eventuality, your servers remain up and running and able to deliver pages to the internet. Datacenters are not perfect. If a tornado drops a house on one, it's likely to be flattened, just like any other building, but having your servers housed in one rather than at your office provides the best possible environment for maintaining server uptime.

2: Finding and targeting a market niche

As with any business, the top two questions you have to ask before even starting to plan your business are:

Who needs my product?

Why would they choose me?

These questions help you to define your market and identify a particular section of the market or 'niche' that is most suitable for you.

Developers/Designers

Many people start out as web hosts because they are working as website developers and find that it is easiest and most convenient if they simply 'host' their clients' websites on their own server. This gives them the maximum amount of control and makes it far easier for them when developing or fixing issues with sites.

In this case the hosting part of their business is very much secondary to their main core, which is the design and development work, so for them answering those two questions is fairly simple.

Who needs their product? **Their clients.**

Why would those clients choose to use them as a web host? **Because it's the easiest and most convenient option available.**

> *"A lot of web designers do not host and are missing the opportunity of recurring revenue. You can compete with the GoDaddy'sof this business because you can offer YOUR support, not someone from a foreign land calling themselves Kevin. You and your client are a team and are in full control of their websites, email, SEO, etc., all done through cPanel and WHMCS. "*
>
> - *Stephen Picardi, Spearhead Multimedia*

Everyone Else

Some people get into the hosting business through other routes though or want to expand their hosting business beyond just their current clients.

If you fall into this group, it is essential to define who you are aiming at. There are a lot of companies already competing in the hosting business and thus, making a mark in the web hosting business and luring clients away from other larger, more established hosts can be quite tricky. Potential clients require some form of incentive or compelling reason to switch providers or to choose you in the first place.

Finding Your Niche

Defining your market, your niche, can be tricky at times, but a good place to start is to look for where you already have influence and contacts, then design and mold your business plan to suit and embrace those contacts.

> *Don't let the market define you, define your market. There are hundreds if not thousands of niches available in web hosting. Find one you like, be great at it and dominate it.*
>
> *- Zach McClung, Jaguar PC*

For small businesses, one of the most powerful forms of advertising these days is social media. Almost every market for every product is oversaturated with suppliers so, increasingly, consumers are turning to recommendations from friends and family as to who the 'best' suppliers are.

Social media presents anyone and everyone the opportunity to easily get in contact with and create friendships with like-minded people all over the world. As these social circles increase, personal recommendations of which companies provide good service and which provide bad service can be shared quickly and easily across large networks of people who have often never met in real life but who still trust and respect each other's opinions.

This is marketing gold for good companies, so finding a niche where you are already visible (where you already have friendships) can help to quickly establish you as a trusted company and kick-start your growth.

We surveyed thousands of hosting companies across the globe and one of the questions we asked was, "What one piece of advice would you give to new hosting startups?"

The response we got overwhelmingly tipped one of two ways.

1) Provide excellent service. Your service and support is what will make or break you.
2) Find your niche and dominate it.

The market is saturated with big companies who offer low prices and just want to suck in as many customers as possible, unless you are extremely well funded, you are not going to be able to compete with them. Instead, become the go-to company in your niche and then expand to other niches when you have that one down.

3: Choosing and provisioning a server

There are essentially three different types of servers that you can use when starting out.

- A shared server (reseller account)
- A VPS
- A dedicated server

Reseller accounts are the entry-level into the hosting world and essentially mean that you are purchasing space and resource on somebody else's shared server and reselling that space to your clients.

This is often a good way to start, although depending on which provider you get your reseller account from, there can be some limitations imposed on you as to how many accounts you can resell and what facilities you can give them. The general idea though is that you would pay a fixed monthly fee for a reseller account and within that account you have the freedom and ability to create sub-accounts for your clients

The next level of server is the VPS, which stands for Virtual Private Server. This is almost like having your very own server, except instead of having a physical box next to you, your host uses virtualization software that splits

up one of their physical servers into a number of 'virtual' ones. Each of these has its own portion of the server's resources allocated to it.

The advantage of a VPS over a shared server is that you (in theory) cannot be slowed down by other people using the server. On a shared server, all the websites hosted on that server vie for the servers' resources. As a reseller on a shared server, you are selling space on a server which could have hundreds or even thousands of other websites hosted on it. If any of those sites starts taking up large amounts of memory or processor time, all the sites on the server slow down.

On a VPS, however, all the resources you can use are allocated solely to you and not shared with other clients. This means that, in theory, nobody else can slow your clients' sites down. The system is not perfect though and this does very much depend on what virtualization software is used and how well it is configured. In some configurations, you sometimes find that virtual servers are allowed some overlap of resources and when one causes the server a problem, sometimes the server's resources are all dragged down. The advantage of a virtual server over a dedicated server however is that it is like having your own miniature dedicated server, which enables you to get out of a shared environment into an en-

vironment where you have a lot of control and have a say on how the server is configured without the cost of paying for a whole physical server for yourself.

A dedicated server is, as its name suggests, a server which is 100% dedicated to you. It is a physical server in a rack in a datacenter which is yours and only yours to use. No-one else has access to it, so you are not sharing anything with anyone. You are then free to do whatever you want with your server, hosting as few or as many clients on it as you wish. You can even install virtualization software on it and set up your own VPS's to use or resell.

This infographic from our friends at InMotion gives a great overview of the differences between the types of servers.

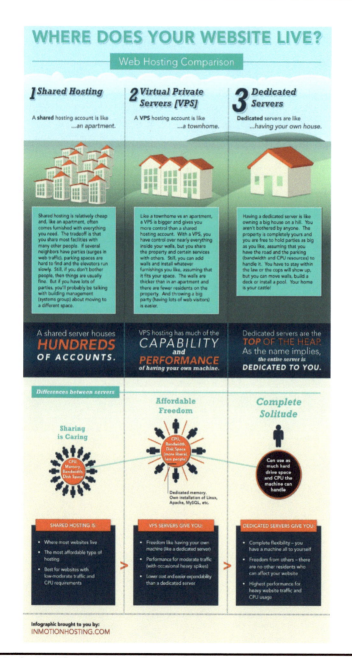

> *Use cPanel. It will make everything a LOT easier, especially if you are new to shared hosting.*
>
> *- Steve Venter, Texo Web Hosting*

Selecting software

Choosing the right server, and the right software to run on that server is essential.

If you start out with a reseller plan, everything is already done for you. Your control panel will be pre-loaded and everything will be ready to roll.

If you start out with a VPS or Dedicated server though, you will have choices to make about what software you wish to run.

The company which supplies your server will normally offer a range of operating systems, control panels (such as cPanel) and configurations for the server and will probably also offer server 'management', which can be invaluable when you are starting out and do not have a full tech team to manage your servers.

Most hosts will have a demo available where you can test out the control panels and software you are thinking of using before committing to them. It's always a good idea to do this before launching as it can be very tricky to switch control panels at a later date.

Managing your business with WHMCS

Don't forget about your billing/management software. Start as you mean to go on, with a well set-up system that will help you from day one and will grow with you as your company grows.

WHMCS is the world's leading web hosting automation platform. Handling customer signups, provisioning, billing and support, WHMCS is used by tens of thousands of web hosting businesses around the world to manage their daily operations and put them firmly in control of their business.

Some of the key benefits are hands free automation, integrated support tools, multi-currency billing, domain management, and much more. More of the benefits of utilizing WHMCS can be found at **http://www.whmcs.com/features**.

If you want to get started you can order WHMCS at **http://www.whmcs.com/order.** Take it from us,

WHMCS will be a life saver when it comes to running your web hosting company efficiently with the powerful automation and excellent features WHMCS has to offer.

Tip: something to consider is hosting your WHMCS installation is on a separate server from where you house your client's sites. That way, your clients can still contact you in the event of an outage.

See Chapter 8 for more details on how to install WHMCS.

4: Selecting a domain registration provider

Selecting a domain name provider can be tricky and confusing, as there are many, many, many, many, many choices of providers out there, whose services vary in quality but have very similar prices.

Knowing the different factors to look for and what makes one provider stand out above the rest can really help as you go about choosing between them.

The first major decision you need to make relates to how many domain names you expect to sell or to register in your first year or two of business.

Resell domains

If you don't expect to sell thousands of domains immediately, then you probably don't need to go to the expense of becoming a registrar. You can simply register as a reseller with one of the registrars that are already out there. To register is a quick process and here are some of the things you need to think about as you're picking a provider.

Probably the most important factor for most people will be the ability to integrate with the software you're using

---

for your hosting management. WHMCS provides a lot of options and already integrates well with a lot of providers - and in fact the software allows any domain registrar to integrate with them providing the registrar has an API and you find someone to write the integration code.

The next thing you need to look at is the cost of registering domain names, but here's the catch: depending on the registrar you choose, domain names for different geographic regions can vary wildly in cost. You need to work out which country(s) you expect to be doing the most business in (which will tell you the domain extension you should expect to be registering the most) and find a company that will give you a good deal on those names. For example, if most of your business is going to be in the UK, going with the provider that gives the best deals on .com registrations might be false economy because their .co.uk registrations may be much higher than elsewhere.

A lot of domain registrars require upfront deposits to get their best pricing tiers, but another benefit of choosing WHMCS as your automation software is that you get access to better pricing without having to commit to any upfront costs.

WHMCS has partnered with **ResellerClub** and **Enom** to get you great deals when you sign up as a reseller with them. Visit **http://whmcs.com/partners** to learn more.

One other thing you should look out for is the cost of transferring domain names away, as this can come as a very unwanted surprise, however you do not have to worry about this with either eNom or ResellerClub. Some registrars will charge you an admin fee for releasing domain names for transfer out. If ever one of your customers was to change to a different service provider (of course they never would, because you're amazing) then you could be charged a fee to allow them to leave. It is not extremely common practice in the industry but it's a hidden fee to check for in advance.

Become a registrar

If you're realistically looking in the thousands of domains, there may well be a good business case for becoming a domain name registrar.

There is a significantly higher startup cost to becoming a registrar, but it has the advantage of allowing you to

register domain names cheaper (in most cases) and will mean you are not at the mercy of another provider.

You will need to apply to become a registrar for all the TLD's and ccTLD's you wish to sell. This means applying to the internet registry in each country to sell domains with their extension. For example. Nominet in the UK and Verisign in the USA. This makes the startup cost even higher, but there might still be value in it if you are intending on registering vast quantities of domains.

5: Def ning your Hosting Products

Hosting is a product. It may not be a tangible, physical product but it is a product and so you need to define what your product can do and what it can't do.

There are a myriad of functions that a web server can provide, but the question is, which ones will come sup-plied free with your product (the hosting plan) and which will be upgrades or add-ons?

This is your business. It is your choice how you form your hosting plans and, depending on your target mar-ket, hosting plans can look very different. A common practice is to have a scale of plans starting with the least expensive having just the essential facilities etc. moving up the scale to the more expensive and fully featured plans. Of course, if you are just hosting your design cli-ents, you may just want to create one plan for everybody which gives complete and free access to all the server resources. That way you don't have to worry about any artificial limits that you're putting on people's plans - but it is also a good idea to monitor your clients' sites to en-sure that they are not using an undue amount of your server time and space.

Creating the Package

Hosting plans are known as 'packages' within WHM and 'products' in WHMCS. Packages must be created in order to add clients to your server. Without a package, the server would not know what to allow the client access to and what to not allow them access to, so it will not allow you to add a client without first creating at least one package.

Two of the most important things to consider when creating hosting plans are:

1) The amount of bandwidth you allow your clients to use
2) The amount of disk space they are allowed

These items are ones for which you can quantify the cost. You will be paying your host for them and if you use over the amount you are allocated by your server host, you'll have to pay for additional size and space.

For example, if you have purchased a VPS with 40Gb of disk space, which is costing you $40 per month, you are essentially paying $1 per Gb per month or $12 per Gb per year.

If you then charge your customer $50 per year and offer them 20Gb of disk space for that price, you are potential-

ly paying a total of $240 per year for the disk space that you are charging $50 for.

That's not going to make you any money!

Many hosts appear these days to offer unlimited amounts of space and of bandwidth, but financially this is not really viable since space and bandwidth are somewhat fixed costs per megabyte/gigabyte.

In reality, the truth behind many unlimited plans is that they are only unlimited to the degree that a small website may use as much disk and bandwidth resource as it wants - but it is not given an unlimited amount of processor time!

Picture data again in terms of water and pipes:

You can have a reservoir as big as you like and you can have pipes coming from that reservoir that are as big as you want them to be, which can cope with an unlimited amount of water being pumped through them…. But the restriction comes from the pump itself. If you try to demand too much water be pumped out of the reservoir, the water company will complain that you're overloading the pumps and force you to either pump less or pay to upgrade the pumps!

While a site can use as much bandwidth and disk space as it likes, the company will crack down if the user is using large amounts of processing resources - which in effect means they cannot use unlimited bandwidth, because the use of unlimited bandwidth also requires the use of unlimited processor resources!

Processor resources are monitored and, should a client who is on an unlimited plan use too much processor time, they will be encouraged to move up from a shared plan to a virtual private server, or even a dedicated server, depending on what would seem best for the website.

Of course, the amount of space and bandwidth you allow the client is often no reflection on the actual amount they use. You can give them 100Gb of disk space, but if their site only needs 1Gb, that's all they will ever use.

After hosting a few websites for a little while, you will begin to get a feel for how much resource an average website for your typical client uses, but in general terms we find that the average small site uses:

- less than 2 GB of disk space
- maybe 400 to 500 MB of bandwidth per month

When sites get more popular, they may jump to using 5, 10 or even 20 GB of bandwidth per month, but the amount of disk space they use very often does not increase in proportion to the amount of bandwidth. This is because bandwidth is measured by the number of page views, not by the number of pages created. As the site becomes more popular, each created page generates more page views and thus uses more bandwidth, even though it's not using any more disk space.

Other things you have to decide on when creating a hosting plan include items such as:

- Email addresses. How many email addresses is each domain name given?
- How many databases they can create
- How many FTP accounts they can have

It is quite common for an arbitrary figure of 100 email addresses and 100 FTP accounts to be given. It's highly unlikely that your customers will use anywhere near that many though. On a shared server, most if not all of your customers are going to be individuals and small businesses and are never going to need more than a handful of each.

Giving a number which sounds generous benefits you by giving a positive perception of what you're offering, but does not realistically change the number of such addresses that will be used.

As you're creating your hosting plan you do have the power to control things to the point of not giving them any email addresses and denying all sorts of features including databases statistics programs etc. etc. which will enable you to control how your clients are using a server how much they can slow it down etc. etc.

The list of main options which are configured in each package include:

✓ Disk quota (MB) ✓ Monthly bandwidth (MB) ✓ Max FTP Accounts ✓ Max Email Accounts ✓ Max Email Lists ✓ Max Databases ✓ Max Sub Domains ✓ Max Parked Domains	✓ Max Addon Domains ✓ Maximum Hourly Email by Domain Relayed ✓ Maximum percentage of failed or deferred messages a domain may send per hour ✓ Dedicated IP ✓ Shell Access

Other features which can be switched on or off for each
domain include:

✓ API Shell (for developers)	✓ Mysql
✓ Ability to Change MX Record	✓ Optimize Website
✓ Addon Domain Manager	✓ Parked Domain Manager
✓ Advanced DNS Zone Editor	✓ Password Change
✓ Analog Stats	✓ PhpMyAdmin
✓ Apache Handlers Manager	✓ PhpPgAdmin
✓ Autoresponder Manager	✓ PostgresSQL
✓ Awstats Stats	✓ R1Soft Restore Backups
✓ Backup Manager	✓ Raw Access Logs
✓ Bandwidth Stats	✓ Ruby on Rails
✓ BoxTrapper Spam Trap	✓ SSH Connection Window
✓ Custom Error Pages	✓ SSL Host Installer
✓ Default Address Manager	✓ SSL Manager
✓ Disk Usage Viewer	✓ Server Status Viewer
✓ Email Account Manager	✓ Simple Cgi Wrapper
✓ Email Archiving	✓ Simple DNS Zone Editor
✓ Email Authentication	✓ Site Software
✓ Email Domain Forwarding	✓ SpamAssassin
✓ File Manager	✓ SpamAssassin Spam Box
✓ Forwarder Manager	✓ Statistics Program Manager
✓ Ftp Account Manager	✓ Subdomain Manager
✓ Ftp Settings	✓ Video Tutorials
✓ Logaholic Web Analytics	✓ Virus Scanner
✓ Mailman List Manager	✓ Webalizer Stats
✓ Mime Types Manager	✓ Webmail

The important thing here though is making sure that your packages include at least as much resource as your target clients will need. People will not switch to you for their hosting if your plans give them less than they know they already use!

6: Setting up Accounts

Once you have a server and a way to register domain names, you can start figuring out how to link the two together and create accounts for your customers. There are four basic steps to doing this:

Register the domain name. As discussed earlier in this book, domain names must be registered through a registrar or third-party registration company

Set the nameservers on the domain to point to your server. Creating nameservers is a part of provisioning your server. Your host will be able to tell you what your nameservers are.

Create the account within WHMCS. Enter the client's details, select the server they will be on and the package they are purchasing and enter the domain name. Before creating your first account, you must input the details of your server, your hosting packages and your domain registrar to your WHMCS system. Do this through the Setup menu.

Email the login details of the account you just created to your client. WHMCS is configured to send an automatic email to the client with these details. There are times when the client will lose these details and they can

---

be resent from within WHMCS. And that's all there is to it. Most of the hard work is done when you set up the server initially and you create a package as described in Chapter 5. Creating new user accounts is simply a matter of pointing the domain name at the server and creating an account with one of the packages that you already set up.

OR

If you wish to integrate your client set up with your billing system, you can automate the set up of the account on your server through the billing system (WHMCS) and here's how the procedure works:

The customer submits an order through a form you place on your website, detailing the new domain name and which hosting plan they wish to be on.

When the customer makes the payment for the new plan, the WHMCS system automatically creates the user account for that domain on your server and then generates an email to the customer giving all the details of how to access the account, including the username and password. This requires no manual input from you or any of your team!

WHMCS can also be set to take the order and not automatically create the account, if you wish to review and approve accounts before allowing them to be created. Once you have reviewed them, the system will automatically create the user's account and send the email.

Creating an account on the cPanel server creates a folder for that domain name, which is only accessible by that user. Within that folder there are various other folders including a folder called public_html. The public_html folder is the folder which will be visible to the Internet, so that will be where they place their web pages.

Once the nameservers are set to the correct names to point to your server and you have created the accounts as above, within 48 hours the name registration, or change, should have propagated around the Internet and the domain will be recognized worldwide. In reality, name propagation is much faster than that (often within minutes) but it could take up to 48 hours.

If you happen to need help getting your business up and running, WHMCS has several services to help you get going. Some of the services are installation, configuration and integration. More information on these can be found at **https://www.whmcs.com/services/**.

7: Receiving Payments

We all love getting paid - and in any business cash flow is always a major issue, especially when your cash flow is not on the positive side.

With a web hosting business your costs are fairly fixed. You know how much your server is going to cost you every month and, if you need to add another server, you know in advance how much adding a server will cost you.

You therefore have a pretty good idea of what your out-goings will be, but what about income? How will you receive payment from your clients?

You can be sure that if you don't pay for your server on time, your host will switch it off very quickly – and your customers will be shouting at you. Your customers, like most customers though, will most likely be very difficult to extract money from - unless you make them pay up-front.

WHMCS can accommodate any payment schedule you might prefer, whether you choose to register your clients' domain name and set up their accounts before they send you any money, having faith in them that they will send the money as promised, or whether you want to

ensure that you have the cash in your pocket before they receive any services from you is totally up to you.

WHMCS can automate switching off/on accounts when they are not paid on time. You can set WHMCS to suspend an account when payment is overdue, meaning that the client's website(s) will go offline. The system will then automatically unsuspend the account when the payment is made and the client's sites will automatically go back online.

Likewise, if you want to set up a monthly/quarterly/yearly payment plan, WHMCS can manage that for you and automatically suspend customers for non-payment.

In these days of Internet transactions and online banking, it is fairly easy to get almost all of your customers to pay in advance using a credit/debit card or bank transfer, depending on which you prefer. What you need to be able to receive these payments is called a payment gateway.

A payment gateway is a service provider that authorizes payments and brokers the transaction between you, your customer, and your customer's credit card company. They are a way for your business to be able to take your customers' credit card details and use them to get

the appropriate payment into your bank account. One of the most well-known payment gateways is PayPal, which most people are familiar with, but there are many others.

Decision time

When selecting a payment gateway, the first thing you need to decide is whether or not you yourself wish to be responsible for your clients credit card details.
If you use a third party gateway like PayPal to receive payments, the customer only gives their credit card details to PayPal. You never see their credit card number at all.

PayPal, as the intermediary, processes the card and sends the money to you.

While this has its advantages, it has the disadvantage of making recurring billing more difficult and gives you less control.

Some other services, such as services provided by your bank may require you to store the credit card details in your own database and thus give you the responsibility of securing and protecting those details.

Many people find that it is simply too risky to store clients' credit card details themselves for fear that a hacker

may get in and steal those details, so they prefer to use a gateway such as PayPal to insulate them from that security risk. There are, however, there are newer systems such as tokenized gateways which offer something of a middle ground. These systems mean you do not have to give up all control of the transactions, but still don't have to store the card details yourself.

WHMCS can work with almost any payment gateway by use of what's known as an API.

API's allow two systems to interact with each other. WHMCS comes with modules built in which can communicate with API's for the major payment gateways. If WHMCS does not have a module for your chosen gateway, you or your web designer may be able to write one to connect the two systems.

Payment gateways already supported include:

 PayPal is the fast, easy, secure way to accept credit cards PayPal, and Bill Me Later® online. Whether your customers shop on PCs or mobile devices, PayPal optimizes the experience to help you capture more sales. Plus, when you add PayPal as a payment option, you add trust and credibility to your site and can tap into millions of active buyers who look for the PayPal way to pay. **Learn more about how PayPal can help your business here**.

e-onlinedata processes credit cards for virtually every size and type of business. By selecting e-onlinedata as your merchant account provider you will receive some of the most competitve rates around backed by leading class support. e-onlinedata is fully integrated into WHMCS to allow you to get the most out of your account. **Click here to find out more.**

Skrill Skrill is one of the world's largest online payment providers currently being used by over 135,000 merchants. With one easy connection you can instantly enter new markets and grow your business. Skrill lets you pay and get paid globally without revealing your financial details. Your free Skrill account remembers everything for you, so your information is always protected and never revealed. **Learn more about Skrill here.**

2Checkout.com (2CO) is a worldwide leader in payment and e-commerce services. Since 2000, 2CO has helped hundreds of thousands of online merchants with a global platform of payment methods and world-class fraud prevention service, hosted on a safe, secure, and reliable PCI-compliant payment system. **Visit the 2CO site to learn more.**

We also support many other Merchant, Tokenization and Third Party gateways. For the full list, **visit http://docs.whmcs.com/Payment_Gateways**

WHMCS is able to be configured to work with multiple gateways and multiple methods of payment to give your customers choice. For instance, giving your clients the primary option to pay via PayPal is ideal, but you can also offer a secondary option of paying by check, for example, and set the system rules to cover what to do in either eventuality.

The important thing to remember though is to make it easy for your customers to pay you. Income is vital to your business, so taking the stress out of making payments will help you immensely.

8: Setting up WHMCS

Installing and configuring WHMCS is a painless process, however it does requires you to complete a few steps. Missing any one of these steps can result in your WHMCS installation not functioning correctly, so ensuring that you follow the guide through all the way is essential.

If you don't want to do it yourself, WHMCS's installation team can do it for you, just visit **http://www.whmcs.com/services/installation/** to order the installation service.

If you want to do the installation yourself, WHMCS has a number of resources on their website at **http://docs.whmcs.com/Installing_WHMCS** including a video which walks you through the entire process. Alternatively, you can follow these instructions (you will need to use an FTP client for some of the steps):

1) Visit **http://download.whmcs.com/**
2) Click the Download button under the Full Release heading - this will be the latest release version
3) Unzip the contents of the zip file you just downloaded to a folder on your computer

4) In that folder, rename the file configura-tion.php.new to configuration.php

5) Upload the entire whmcs folder to your website using an FTP client - if you experience problems, contact the WHMCS technical support team for further assistance.

6) Next rename the folder on your website to what-ever you like (billing, clients, etc...)

7) Now visit the installation script at http://www.yourdomain.com/whmcs/install to run the installer process (change the /whmcs/ part to the folder name you selected in step 6 - if you get an Ioncube related error message you will need to install Ioncube on your server. Con-tact your web hosting provider for assistance with this if necessary.

8) Follow the instructions on screen to install which will involve setting file permissions as listed be-low, entering your license key and setting up your primary admin account

9) When complete, delete the install folder from your web server and CHMOD the configura-tion.php file back to 644.

10) Check that the following file permissions are set correctly:

/ configuration.php CHMOD 400 Readable
/ attachments CHMOD 777 Writeable
/ downloads CHMOD 777 Writeable
/ templates_c CHMOD 777 Writeable

Conf gure your install

The next step is to start configuring your installation
with your regional settings, business details, server details and products for sale. Here are the steps you need
to take for that:

1) Login to the Admin Area and configure your
   General Settings (Setup > General Settings).
   There are multiple tabs under the General Settings, you will want to go through each individ-
   ually and fill out all the necessary details for your
   business. More information can be found on
   WHMCS's documentation at:
   http://docs.whmcs.com/Configuration

2) Setup your Payment Gateways (Setup > Payment
   Gateways). There are multiple payment gateways to choose from. You will need to select the
   gateway that works best for your business. You
   can view a full list of the available payment

gateways at:

http://docs.whmcs.com/Payment_Gateways

3) Setup your Products & Services (Setup > Products and Services). WHMCS has a guide on how to create your first product in the WHMCS system at

http://docs.whmcs.com/Setting_Up_Your_First_Product

4) Configure your Domain Pricing (Setup > Domain Pricing). You need to setup all the TLDs you want to offer, their features & pricing. A guide is available on how to do this specifically at:

http://docs.whmcs.com/Domain_Pricing

5) Setup your Support Ticket Departments (Setup > Support Departments). You can view the documentation on how to setup departments and assign staff to a departments at

http://docs.whmcs.com/Support_Departments

6) Setup email piping so you can manage tickets using the WHMCS Support Desk - for full instructions on this please see the Email Piping article here: **http://docs.whmcs.com/Email_Piping**

7) Ensure the WHMCS Cron Job is setup and configure automated tasks (Setup > Automation Settings). You can find more specific details on how

to setup the necessary cron jobs to automate
WHMCS at: **http://docs.whmcs.com/Crons**

8) Place some test orders on your website to check
everything works as expected

There are plenty of other settings you can change to customize your WHMCS install to your exact requirements,
but those listed above are the important ones to get you
started.

**Tip: Perform the recommended Further Security Steps
listed here:**
http://docs.whmcs.com/Further_Security_Steps

Customize your site

You may also want to customize the WHMCS customer-
facing screens to match your current website. These cus-
tomizations can be done easily by a web designer, or
you can use our customization service and have us do
the work for you. Visit
http://www.whmcs.com/services/integration/ for more
details.

9: Legal Documents

Legal documents. We all hate them and we all wish we never had to see another one again. For the business owner though, they are essential in protecting you, your staff and your business from vengeful customers and possible future legal problems.

Ensure that you hire a lawyer who has experience working with legal documents for the tech industry.

We all see and don't bother to read terms and conditions and other legal documents all the time. You have to accept all kinds of different things to install software and most of us never have any idea what we're actually agreeing to, we just check the box and click on through.

Those legal documents lay out the seller's liabilities, obligations and options and protect the seller's rights.

The long and the short of it is that you need to have rock-solid legal documents on your websites for everybody to see, which protect you against the people out there who don't want to take responsibility for the problems they cause and would rather sue someone instead. These documents need to clearly limit your liabilities and very thoroughly show what your responsibilities are in hosting your clients' websites.

Your terms and conditions also need to reflect your business ethics - to give you the authority and capability of refusing to house any websites that you don't wish to house.

Yes, it's quite likely that at some point somebody is going to want to host their new porn site on your server, or their website promoting their favorite political figure or whatever it may be. You will see it and just feel you cannot stomach having your business be any part of it, even if you're only providing the hosting.

Your terms and conditions need, from the very beginning, to state what kinds of sites or kinds of content you don't allow so, when you discover them you can remove them, or even better, the client sees that you don't allow them before purchasing and never even tries.

Of course, there's the law to consider. It may be that the law in your region or country prohibits you from rejecting any websites based on grounds such as political affiliation or religion, so ensuring that your terms and conditions not only protect you the way you want to be protected from your clients but are also in line with the law of the land means you really can't avoid it – you're going to have to hire a lawyer.

Sorry.

A lawyer will be able to assist you in complying with the laws of the country you're in and with knowing what is required from businesses in that country. They will also be able to provide you with the wording necessary for the documents that you must have on your website.

The lawyer will also be able to tell you what, if any, information must be disclosed at the time of sale so that you can ensure that you require your customers to read and agree to whatever they need to before purchasing from you.

Examples of the types of documents you may need are:

- Terms and conditions of sale
- Terms of service
- Privacy Policy

With these essential documents in place, you can feel more confident about your company's legal protection as you start to bring in clients.

Do not put off ensuring that you have your terms and conditions etc. correct and on your website.

Some companies never have legal action taken against them, but some companies may find that their very first client is the one who decides to sue!

Do not take the need for these documents too lightly. They are for your protection.

10: Addons and upsells

> *Hosting alone is a low margin business, bundle
> hosting with other services to add value and
> margin.*
>
> — *Phil Eschallier, 10 Types, Inc*

The question is often asked, "How do you make money
as a web host?"

Margins are tight and there are companies out there who
seem to charge so little for hosting sites that it seems
they must be making a loss, yet they are successful and
growing.

The answer is simple: addons and upsells are where the
profit is.

Upselling is the art of showing the customer enhanced
services and demonstrating to them that they need to
purchase those services.

McDonalds is famous for their use of the upsell with the
line, "do you want fries with that?" Just that simple
question asked by every one of its employees all around
the world generated millions in extra profit.

Car dealerships are well known for it too. Salesmen often make more commission from selling extended warranties, service contracts and even arranging financing than they do from the actual sale of the car.

Web hosting gives you the opportunity to sell a wide variety of addons and upgrades. Here are just a few of them that other hosts have found to be profitable.

SSL certificates. Web security is a hot topic and any website where financial transactions take place needs an SSL certificate. An SSL certificate proves to your customer that your site is legitimate and adds security to the transaction. There are a number of different companies which offer certificates and a number of different levels of security offered. Check out our page on protecting your own website with an SSL certificate at **http://www.whmcs.com/ssl-certificates**. As a host, you can also resell certificates to your clients with a fairly high profit margin – and make the same profit every year when the certificate is renewed. The help page on WHMCS's website shows you how to easily configure WHMCS to sell SSL certificates and even has a video tutorial: **http://docs.whmcs.com/Enom_SSL_Certificates**

TRUSTe Privacy Policies. Every website needs a privacy policy and Truste are a great place to get one. Using a WHMCS module, you can resell TRUSTe privacy policy products to your clients and help them gain greater trust from their website users.

Server upgrades. Helping your customers see the benefits of upgrading to a VPS or Dedicated server helps both them and you. The extra speed, security and flexibility gained by upgrading to a VPS or Dedicated server is a great benefit to the client and the higher cost of those servers means more profit for you. Two great solutions for creating a VPS are **SolusVM** and **OnApp**. Both have great integration with WHMCS and are both powerful and easy to use. Find out more about them at **http://docs.whmcs.com/SolusVM** and **http://onapp.com/whmcs**

Dedicated IP Addresses. Even customers with a shared hosting account can benefit from a dedicated IP address. Many firms who run 'blacklist' services to block sites which are sending spam or delivering malware don't just block the troublesome site, they block the entire IP address that site is on. This means that every website which shares that IP address (commonly all sites on a shared server) will find themselves blocked regardless of

whether or not they are at fault. For a small amount per
month, you can offer your clients their own, dedicated
IP address, to give them some protection from this, even
though they are still on the same server.

Design/Development. Some clients will want to devel-
op their own websites. Many will need help though.
There are many, many designers they can go to, but
since they're already connected with you as their host,
why not become a one-stop-shop for them and provide
design and development services. If your niche market
includes a lot of bloggers, offering WordPress support
and customization services can be very profitable, too.

Backups. Although backups are vitally important, many
website owners have no backup of their website at all.
Many are willing to pay for a nightly backup (which you
should, ideally, be doing yourself anyway) so it can generate an extra revenue stream at little or no cost to you.

Managed Services. As your clients move up to using
VPS and Dedicated Server solutions, so the
technical day-to-day management of those servers becomes more difficult for them. You could offer different
levels of server management to your clients depending
on what they will require, all the way from no management to managing every detail of their server – for a fee.

Domain ID Protection. Domain name records are public records, which means anyone can search for a domain name and see not only who owns that domain but what their email address is and even sometimes their mailing address and phone number.ID protection is offered by most registrars as a resell add-on to mask the true owner's details and protect them from trolls searching the net for domain owners to try to scam.

DNS Management. WHMCS provides the facility to limit which DNS management features your clients can access and sell additional management options as add-ons. Instead of giving all of your clients access to everything, which most of them don't need, you can configure the system so that clients who want greater DNS management flexibility can purchase the additional features.

11: Technical support - inside or outside

From day one as a web host, you'll find yourself needing to answer technical support queries from your clients. These queries will vary from the mundane, seemingly obvious kinds of questions all the way up to more head-scratchingly difficult ones.

Some of the queries will actually relate to the hosting itself, but others will relate to the users' website and not be related to the hosting at all.

> *Support, Support, Support. The most important piece of any hosting company is their support.*
>
> *- Cameron Allen, SohoLaunch.com*

Some will be easy to answer, some may take some time and some digging - but all of them need to be answered one way or another.

So... the question is, who do you want to delegate as the one who is answering all of these questions?

Do you want it to be you? Do you have a team that can handle tech-support questions? Will your business model support you employing a team from the very begin-

ning? Questions will arise from day one and you need to know who and how to get the answers before you even start.

There are a variety of different ways to accomplish this:

Do-it-yourself. If your client base is likely to be small or, in fact, your clients are not going to be getting involved in the hosting at all, because you are developing the sites for them and intending to do all the management of the hosting as well, doing it yourself can be a very good way to go.

Hire support staff. If you have more than just a few clients, answering all the questions may take more time than you're able to dedicate to them, so you could hire your own in-house team. An in-house team could start as just one person. Unless you are certain that you will have an influx of customers, it's unlikely that you'll need more than one support person initially and you can always add to your team as becomes necessary.

Outsource. The last (but not least) option is to outsource your support by using one of a number of third-party support organizations. This can be a very effective way to provide support to your clients, but it can also be costly, so you will need to calculate carefully upfront what

the actual cost of support per user is going to be - and build that into the cost of the product you sell.

If you're thinking of outsourcing support, one question you may want to consider is how it will affect upsells and add-ons and whether it would, in fact, cause you to lose valuable additional business that you may be able to generate by having a personal relationship with your clients.

Support Desk is Now Closed

Another factor to consider is what times of day your clients are going to be requesting support and how you provide support at all those times

> *Be available 24/7 for your clients. There is a lot of hand holding to do.*
>
> *- Dave Ferri, Orchard Studio/Hosting/TV*

In this day and age, most businesses are not 9-to-5 businesses anymore and your customers will get very unhappy if they find that they can't get support from you after 5 o'clock in the evening or before 9am.

Although their websites may not have a high amount of traffic, it is still important for them that their website be available as much of the time as possible, particularly if

their website is advertising or selling a product or service. 21st Century online customers can come at any time of day or night and if they find a website is not available, may well never come back, causing a loss of business - and nobody wants that.

> *Always go the extra mile for your customers, they will return it four fold in extra business, referrals and great reviews.*
>
> *- Paul Nesbitt, PAC Web Hosting*

So you have to think about, if you are providing support in-house, how you provide that support outside of normal working hours and outside of the normal work week, such as the weekends and public holidays. With an outsourced support solution, 24/7/365 is not so much of a problem, but if you're doing the support personally or have to pay someone else to work nights and weekends, your costs could spiral out of control quickly.

Customer Service Philosophy

Every company has developed its own customer service philosophy, with some more loved by clients than others.

More than anything else, your company is going to be measured by how well it communicates with and sup-

ports its customers. The way and amount that you communicate with the people who are relying on you as their host can dramatically change their perception of you and of your hosting.

Whether your philosophy is one of extremely fast and efficient customer service, or maybe ensuring for every single customer, you go above and beyond the call of duty every single time, it is going to become an integral part of your business and what your company is known for.

They say you never get a second chance to make a first impression and this holds true with customer service and the way you treat your customers. The first time they contact you might also be the last , depending on their expectations and how you live up to them Ensuring that you have a good system in place for recording, monitoring and following through with customer service queries is essential. A system such as the ticket system in WHMCS provides the perfect method of making sure clients and potential clients have their queries answered quickly and they are not forgotten about.

There are shelves and shelves full of books written on how to provide great customer service, but in the end it comes down to this:

Treat your customers the way you would want to be treated.

Or maybe more accurately:

Treat your customers the way THEY want to be treated.

Rudeness, slow responses and a lack of information are universally hated, so if your company displays any of those traits, it may well quickly become universally hated too.

When you are hiring staff, it is very important that they know intimately what your customer service philosophy is so that they can live up to that philosophy and not let you and your company down by doing something different. Just having an idea in your head of how you want your customers to be treated, or even having that idea written down but not taught and consistently reinforced to your employees does not bring that idea to reality.

12: Backups

Backups are essential.

There is no getting around it. You need to take full, regular backups of all of your clients' sites.

The backups are not for the client though, they're for you.

> *Always ensure that you have adequate off site backups of all the accounts on your servers.*
>
> *- Stuart McCulloch, Star Web Hosting*

Many hosts do not include daily backups as part of their standard hosting plan, preferring instead to sell them as an add-on.

That's fine, as long as the customer is fully aware that backups are their own responsibility and are not provided by you, the host.

You should always ensure you have a good backup anyway though. Here's why:

Sometimes, rarely, but sometimes, you or one of your staff is going to do something that messes up a server.

It happens. Even to the best of us.

When that happens, and the issue is clearly your fault, your clients are likely to get at least a little upset – and quite rightly, too.

If you have a backup of their site, you can restore it and smooth the waters fairly easily.

If you DON'T have a backup of their site, you can be sure that they will be loud and boisterous online, spreading the word to everyone that your company likes to screw up servers without taking a backup and leave your customers out to dry.

It's as simple as that. No backup means no safety net for you, which means sooner or later something will happen and you'll start getting some seriously bad press.

How to backup

There are a multitude of different backup systems available, each with their strengths and weaknesses.

Some companies go as far as to take backups hourly (or even less) using software which essentially makes a mirror image of their server.

Most common though is to take a nightly backup, but here's the most important point to remember about taking backups:

MAKE SURE THE BACKUP IS HELD OFFSITE.

Seriously, there are three reasons why a server might fail
and require a restore from a backup:

- Software failure. Whether it's due to hackers,
  something wrong with the software you're running or user error, software issues can wipe sites
  in seconds.
- Hardware failure. It happens. Even the best
  hardware, put together by the best installers goes
  wrong sometimes – and when it does, it usually
  like to do it catastrophically!
- External issues. So your server is in a data center.
  That building has backup generators, fire systems, multiple internet connections, the whole
  works. GREAT. What happens if a freak flood
  washes it away though? Is it built to withstand
  that? Nope. Didn't think so.

Reason #2 above is fairly individual. A hardware failure
catastrophic enough to cause data loss is rarely something that affects more than one server at once.

The other two though are more inclusive and will generally affect multiple machines.

If your backup is held in the server right next to the live server, it's at high risk of being affected by any external issues that affect the live server AND from software issues like hacks or faulty software.

Don't risk it, just keep your backup offsite. It's best for you, your customers and your business as a whole.

13: Launching Your Website

Launching your website can be the most exciting and nerve-wracking part of the process of starting your hosting business.

It's crunch time, the moment of truth, the time when you learn whether or not all that hard work you put in was worth it. Don't be dismayed though if you don't sign a million clients in your first week, this is a competitive industry and it can take a little time to gain a footing.

There are many different ways to market any business, so we asked some already established web hosts for their advice on the best way to ensure that your launch is a success.

Here is just some of the advice they shared from their past experiences.

- Market to local small businesses by:
    - Telephone
    - Going door-to-door
    - Joining local business associations
    - Newspaper
    - Mail campaign
    - Social media campaigns
    - ebay

- Be active on hosting forums (such as webhosting-talk)
- Have sales representatives on commission
- Facebook Ads
- Google Adwords
- Shape the messaging of the campaign around how easy and painless hosting with your company is. Comparing prices, megabytes, gigabytes, subdomains etc. just confuses most decision makers who are looking for hosting.
- Have a simple and effective website builder
- Design a free site or two for clients who will shout your praises to everyone they meet, or at least really cheap and work word of mouth
- Offer a discount for the first year then maintain the client with quality service.
- Referral and affiliate marketing
- Go where your niche is. Forums, conferences etc. to meet people and spread the word about your service
- Become a sponsor of conferences for your niche market
- Advertise in magazines your market would read
- Work with some designers to host their clients' websites

- Offer free website design with hosting plans and advertise it on the local newspaper
- TV and Radio ads - if you have the budget.
- Run contests
- Make 'how to' Youtube videos to build an audience to whom you can advertise
- Offer a free transfer service. The pain of transferring everything over can be a major reason why people don't switch hosts.

These are just some ideas to get you started. Interestingly, there are some things which certain hosts have found to work really well for them, which other hosts have found to be a complete marketing failure.

Don't limit yourself to one marketing strategy, try a few different avenues and see what works best for your business. It may take a few tries to find which forms of advertising are best for you, so DON'T GIVE UP. Your perfect campaign is out there somewhere, you just have to find it!

14: Selling Your Hosting Business

Typically new hosting startups fall into one of two categories:

- you are entering the hosting business with the aim of doing it for the rest of your life
- you're entering it with the aim of creating a profitable business to sell

Either way it is smart to, from the very start, think about what makes a hosting business viable to sell and what potential buyers will be looking for.

We interviewed Hillary Stiff from Cheval Capital to find out what acquisitions specialists look for when buying hosting companies. Her answers, while being excellent for anyone looking to sell their hosting company, also make great business sense for ANY organization, whether it's looking to sell or not.

When a hosting company is looking to buy another company, there are some major things that can make the purchase look attractive and some which can put buyers off in an instant.

Hillary explained that there is no one-size-fits-all formula to use, but she outlined some of the most common pluses and minuses and why they are important.

Major Plus Points

When looking to acquire another company, unless the acquisition is strategic, one of the biggest factors that a company will look at is the ease of transfer. Here are some things which make transfers easier:

Using an industry standard control panel. cPanel is the most commonly used control panel and contains easy tools to help migrate accounts from one server to another. When integrating your clients into another existing infrastructure, ease of transition is paramount. The same goes for the billing/management software. Using a popular system like WHMCS makes it easier for customer details to be shifted over to the buyer's systems.

Up to date equipment and infrastructure.. There may be a period after the acquisition when the buyer has to use your servers and the systems you have in place, before they can transfer all of the clients over to their systems. Using current, standard equipment makes it both easier for their technical department to maintain your systems during that process and to migrate everything across.

Well separated billing/accounting/technical infrastructure for different products, so they could be sold separately. For example, both the Web TV creation side of your business and the hosting side may be viable businesses to sell, but a prospective buyer may only want to buy one side of the business. If the two are too intertwined, it may not be easy, or even possible to separate the two out, making them much harder to sell.

Good brand recognition/a positive image. A company is not looking to just buy your customers from you, they are looking to buy a brand that they can be proud of, that will enhance their own reputation. They want to be able to proudly say that your brand is now part of their business and they don't want to be associated with something negative.

Positive growth. This is linked with the previous item, a positive image. If your sales are declining, then there's going to be a reason for that – and it may be something that will reflect badly on the buyer. Selling at a time while your company is still thriving is much easier than waiting until everything is falling apart.

Good financials and a well-organized back office. They don't want you to give them a shoebox full of receipts and invoices that they have to trawl through to sort out

what's what. A well maintained, structured system is much more preferable – and WHMCS helps with that.

An easy transaction. The loan shark down the street may seem like the only way you can raise the capital to start your hosting business, but a future buyer is going to be very wary of buying a company where there are legal, tax or lender issues. If a future buyer is not going to think that a contract you're entering into makes good business sense, then that's a good indication that you should steer clear of it – for your own good!

Major Minus Points

Obviously most of the minuses are just the reverse of the pluses, but it bears listing them for clarity:

Declining revenues. Sometimes a business can be valuable to acquire even though it has fallen on hard times, but generally speaking, you need to sell while the going is good. Don't wait too long!

High customer churn. Customers come and customers go. It's inevitable in any business that a percentage of customers will not renew their contract at the end of the year. However, if a large proportion of customers are jumping ship every year, then that's going to be a red flag to your buyer.

Selling the customers without the brand. Here's where some forethought has to come into how you brand your business. Integrating your new hosting business with your current, well known, brand might seem like good business sense now, but what happens when you want to sell just the hosting side and not give up the brand name? Not being able to buy the positive attributes of a good brand will make the deal very much less attractive to the buyer.

Being disorganized and unresponsive. Think about it for a moment. If you want another company to pay you top dollar for the company you own, seeming like you don't know what you're doing, or not having the courtesy to respond promptly to queries and requests is going to seriously put them off. Don't forget, you need them more than they need you!

A 'hairy' transaction. Make everything clean, legal and totally above board. Prospective buyers will run for the hills if you have long leases they won't be able to get out of, high debts and other liabilities.

Technology/software/control panels that are outdated, proprietary or incompatible with others. Don't forget, the purchaser is not buying you out because they want to run two separate companies, they're buying you out

so they can integrate the two businesses together. If your setup is hard for them to integrate with/migrate to their current systems, it can make the purchase less attractive or even unviable.

Valuation

All of the plus and minus points to making your company viable to sell, also affect its valuation. The bulk of business acquisitions in the hosting industry are consolidations, where an already established hosting business is looking to buy your company and absorb it into its business structure.

These purchasers know how much their servers cost to run and are therefore looking for what your revenues are, so they can see how much profit your business will make for them.

The plus and minus points we've already mentioned therefore raise or lower your company's valuation. For example:

On the plus side, good brand recognition and image may add to the value, whereas a widely disliked brand will reduce the value.

Good customer growth will add to the value, whereas a declining customer base will be much less valuable.

One of the biggest costs involved for the purchaser comes after the purchase, and that is the cost of integrating your customers into their systems. If they can do a quick, easy, automated migration from your systems to theirs, it will be a lot cheaper for them than, for instance, if someone has to manually transfer all the records from your business. The cost to integrate the two businesses will greatly affect the valuation, so the easier you make it for the buyer, the more they are going to be willing to pay!

Metrics

A purchaser will also look at various metrics which will help them get a feel for your business and will affect the value. These metrics include:

Total revenue. Duh.

Monthly revenue per customer. A million dollars a year in revenue may sound good, but if your revenue per customer is only a nickel, the number of customers becomes irrelevant.

Monthly customer churn. How many customers are you losing/gaining every month? If you're gaining a thousand a month but losing a thousand a month too, your business is not growing.

Length of customer term. If you have a lot of customers but they have all paid for five years of hosting up front, your buyer won't see any revenue from those customers for a long time. However, if they are all paying monthly then they will see an immediate revenue stream.

Website analytics. Your customers need to think about SEO and visitor numbers – and so do you. Word-of-mouth sales are good, but good numbers of visitors to your site is very valuable and could affect the valuation of the business quite considerably.

All in all, making your business a good value proposition for potential buyers means from the very start you should be organized and run the business well – two things which make perfect business sense for all companies.

Web hosting is a fast-growing, much needed industry where there is plenty of money to be made and a seemingly inexhaustible number of potential new clients coming to the market every day. WHMCS provides the tools

you need to quickly get your new hosting business set up and ready to roll in a way that will help you to easily and quickly expand and adapt to changing market conditions, while keeping everything running smoothly and efficiently.

Don't let fears and doubts hold you back, but instead know that thousands of other people have started out just like you and found that with WHMCS, the leading web hosting automation platform, they have been able to build a successful, profitable web hosting business – and had fun doing it!

Glossary of terms

Affiliates

An affiliate system is one where a person gets paid a commission for referring clients to someone. In your case, it will be people (your affiliates) referring new customers to you. It can be difficult to keep track of who referred whom and so WHMCS has a tracking system built in which enables you to track where new clients are coming from and pay commissions accordingly.

Nameservers

Nameservers are like a phonebook for the internet to tell internet browsers where to find websites. Every domain name has at least two nameservers associated with it (for redundancy). These nameservers hold a record of the IP address where that domain is hosted. When someone types a domain name into a browser, that browser looks up the domain name's nameservers and queries them to find out which server it needs to visit to find the website for that domain.

Private Nameservers

Any server anywhere in the world can act as a nameserver for any domain. What most hosting companies do is

to provide a server which acts as the name server for all of their clients. For example, if you hosted your domain at Inmotion Hosting, the nameservers for your domain would be ns1.inmotionhosting.com and ns2.inmotionhosting.com. These nameservers then hold a record of the IP address of the actual server your site is on. Private nameservers are a way of masking the fact that your site is hosted by (in this example) Inmotion Hosting and instead use your domain name as the nameserver address, e.g. ns1.yourdomain.com and ns2.yourdomain.com. Private nameservers, also called **vanity nameservers** are easy to set up and can add a little bit of a professional touch to the domain's records.

Propagation

Propagation is the term used to describe the updating of new server information about a domain around the internet. When you change the server that a domain is hosted on, the DNS record for that domain at its nameserver must be updated to reflect the change. Although those changes are very often seen within five minutes, it can take as long as 48 hours for them to take effect worldwide.

POP3

POP3 is a protocol for handling email for a domain. The POP3 protocol allows for email to be downloaded and stored separately from the server by mail clients such as Microsoft Outlook or Mozilla Thunderbird.

IMAP

IMAP is a protocol for handling email for a domain. With the IMAP protocol, emails are held centrally on the mail server and then mirrored to whatever device you are using. Any changes made to the emails on your device are then reflected back to the mail server. The server holds a record of which emails have been read, what has been replied to etc etc. This has the advantage of meaning you can log in from different devices at different times and your mailbox will always be up to date with where you last left it. The disadvantage is that if you delete an important email, it will be gone from every device you read your email on. You won't have the comfort of knowing that you still have a copy of it on another computer.

Recurring Billing

Recurring Billing is where you set up your billing system to automatically charge your clients' credit cards

when their renewal becomes due. This could be monthly, quarterly or yearly but it aids your cash flow by giving more of a guarantee that payments will be made on time – because it takes the onus away from the client to log in and make payment.

Pro-Rata/Pro-Rated Billing

Pro-Rata billing is where you charge someone less than full price, based on how much time is left in the billing period. Pro-rating allows you to synchronize billing periods to make payments easier to manage. For instance, if your customer pays annually for hosting and nine months into the year decide to add daily backups to their hosting plan, you might pro-rate the cost for the remaining three months of the year (charging them ¼ of the full-year rate because they only have ¼ of the year left). When their hosting plan comes up for renewal, you would then charge them for the next full year of hosting and the next full year of backups.

Co-Location Hosting

Co-Location (or colocation) hosting is very similar to dedicated server hosting, in that you have a server all to yourself, it just has one important difference: <u>You provide the server</u>. With other types of hosting, you rent a

server from your host, which they configure and then house within a datacenter of their choice. Colocation cuts out the middle man and means that you buy and configure the server then deliver it to the datacenter, where it is put in a rack with other people's servers. The advantage of colocation is that you get to define, build and configure your own server then connect it to the internet without all the costs of having to build your own secure, data-redundant datacenter with its own backup generators and everything else that goes into ensuring that the server is online 24/7/365.

Dedicated Server Hosting

Dedicated server hosting is where you provide an entire server to a client. They can then do anything they want with it. They are, in effect, just leasing the box from you. The cost to you is obviously significantly higher than shared hosting, but the margins are better and you can sell add-on services such as server management.

VPS

VPS (Virtual Private Server) hosting is a step-up from shared hosting and gives the client significantly more server resource and flexibility. The host uses virtualization software to partition up a dedicated server, giving

each partition a certain amount of the server resources. For instance, if the server has 8Gb of ram, the host may split it into 4 virtual servers, each with 2gb ram. Each virtual server runs its own operating system and is almost completely independent of the other virtual servers it shares hosting with. The client essentially gets their own dedicated server without having to pay for a whole physical server.

Cloud Hosting

Cloud hosting is battling to become the new standard in hosting and works in a slightly different way from standard hosting. Instead of assigning each website to a physical server, the physical servers are all linked together and share their resources in what is called 'the cloud'. Websites are then hosted in 'the cloud' and are not confined to using the resources of a single server. This has great advantages in terms of speed but it also requires a slightly different pricing model. Many companies charge monthly depending on how much resource is used by a site, meaning the cost to the client can vary month-to-month depending on their usage.

Cron Jobs

Cron, taken from the Greek word Cronos is a time-based scheduler for tasks you wish to be run on a server. Each task is given a run time and frequency, e.g. at 2am daily, and is stored in the cron as a 'job'.

Merchant Account

A merchant account is a bank account which enables the owner to accept payment via credit or debit card.

Credit Card Gateway

A credit card gateway acts as the intermediary between your website and the credit card companies. It's like the card swipe machines at checkouts in stores and enables the customer to pay you using their credit card number.

Address Verification System

An Address Verification System is the system used to compare the billing address your client gave you on your website to the actual billing address of the credit card. If the two do not match, the card transaction is declined.

Cardholder Verification Value (CVV2)

The CVV2 is a way of verifying the legitimacy of a credit or debit card. It is either a three digit number printed on the back of the card or a four digit number on the front, in the case of American Express cards. The Credit Card Gateway uses this value along with the credit card number to assess whether or not a card has been stolen.

VAT

VAT (Value Added Tax) is a sales tax added to purchases in the United Kingdom. In retail stores VAT is generally already included in the price of each item but for commercial uses, VAT is normally added on at checkout.

FTP Account

FTP (File Transfer Protocol) is the name of the system used to upload and download files between the server and a client's computer. They need to have specific login details to do this and those details are created as what's called an FTP 'account'. cPanel servers can have an unlimited number of FTP accounts. The server logs which account is used to upload and download which files.

Module

A Module within WHMCS is a section of code which has been or can be added in to the WHMCS system to enable it to connect with another system. Modules include the API code necessary to share information in a way that both systems can understand. Modules can be created for new web hosting panels, registrars and payment gateways.

www.ingramcontent.com/pod-product-compliance
Lightning Source LLC
Chambersburg PA
CBHW041150050326
40689CB00004B/715